All Kinds of Ears

by Jackie Thomas

SCHOLASTIC INC.

Photos ©: cover-back cover: Graham Hatherley/Minden Pictures; 2-3: WLDavies/iStockphoto; 4-5: W. Layer/Blickwinkel/age fotostock; 6-7: DmitryND/iStockphoto; 8-9: vlad61/iStockphoto; 10-11: Fabio Pupin/Minden Pictures; 12-13: Cisca Castelijns/Minden Pictures/Superstock, Inc.; 14-15: Alan and Elaine Wilson; 16: DmitryND/iStockphoto.

No part of this publication may be reproduced in whole or in part, or stored in a retrieval system, or transmitted in any form or by any means, electronic, mechanical, photocopying, recording, or otherwise, without written permission of the publisher. For information regarding permission, write to Scholastic Inc., 557 Broadway, New York, NY 10012.

Copyright © 2018 by Scholastic Inc.
All rights reserved. Published by Scholastic Inc.
Printed in the U.S.A.
Produced by Dinardo Design.

ISBN-13: 978-1-338-26317-6
ISBN-10: 1-338-26317-X

SCHOLASTIC and associated logos are trademarks and/or registered trademarks of Scholastic Inc.

5 6 7 8 9 10   40   26 25 24 23 22

Some animals have big ears to hear.

Some animals have big ears.
Some animals have small ears to hear.
And some animals hear with no ears at all!

African Elephant

This fox has very big ears.

Fennec Fox

This fox lives in a hot place.
Big ears help keep the fox cool.

This fox has small ears.

Arctic Fox

This fox lives in a cold place. Small ears help keep the fox warm.

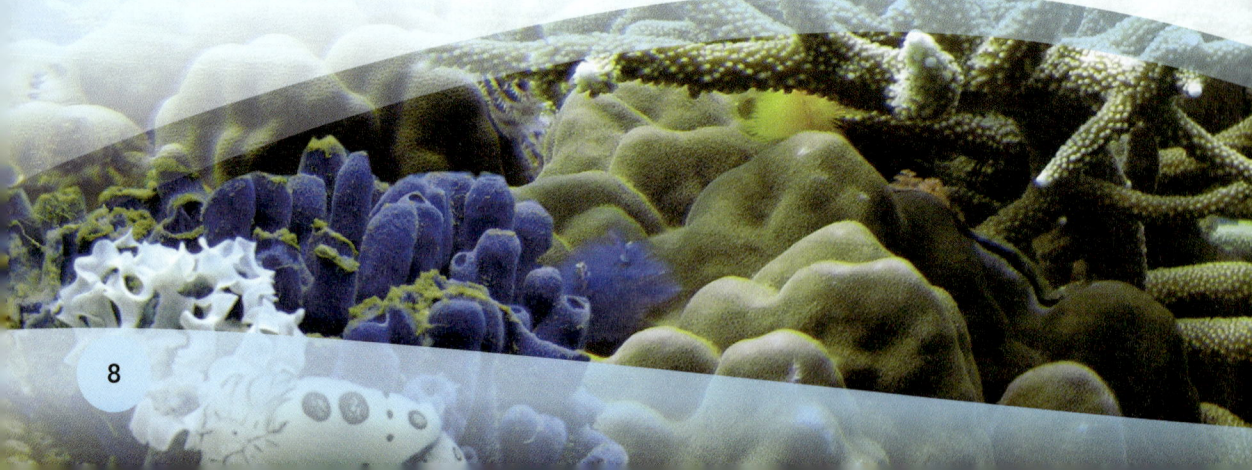

Angelfish

Some animals hear without any ears you can see!

A fish can hear.
But you cannot see its ears.
Its ears are inside its body.

A snake can hear.
But it does not have ears.

Four-lined snake

A snake can feel sounds.

An insect can hear.
But it does not have ears.

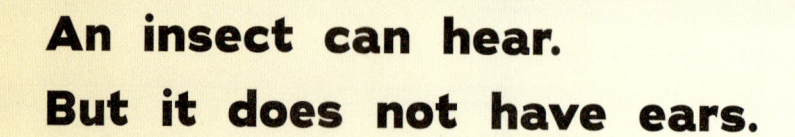

Cricket

An insect uses hairs on its body to feel sound.

A bird can hear.
It has small ears, but they are covered with feathers.

Snowy Owl

How Animals Hear

Big ears
African Elephant
Fennec Fox

Small ears
Arctic Fox
Snowy Owl

No ears
Angelfish
Four-lined Snake
Cricket